A Foot on the Tide

Mary Branley

SUMMER PALACE PRESS

First published in 2002 by

Summer Palace Press
Cladnageeragh, Kilbeg, Kilcar, County Donegal, Ireland

Printed by Nicholson & Bass Ltd.

A catalogue record for this book is available
from the British Library

ISBN   0   95359   12   9   8

This book is printed on elemental chlorine-free paper

for Maggie Wade

Acknowledgments

Some of the poems in this book have previously appeared in *THE SHOp; Cyphers;* Vol. 4 *Field Day Anthology of Irish Writing* (2002) and *Poetry Ireland*. Extracts from 'Quintet' featured on the Arts Zone Literary Tour Lyric FM in September 2000.

Special thanks to Leland Bardwell for her meticulous scrutiny of the text and her invaluable advice.

Biographical Note
Mary Branley was born in Sligo in 1962. After graduating from St. Patrick's College of Education, she taught in Sligo, Boston and London. She completed an MEd in Intercultural Education at Emmanuel College, Boston, in 1992. She co-wrote *Silk Kimonos*, which was performed in the Factory Performance Space, Sligo, in 1995. After eleven years she returned to Sligo and is a Visiting Teacher for Travellers in the Northwest. She is a member of the Scriobh Literary Festival Committee. *Charlie Barley and all his friends*, an anthology of Traveller children's nursery rhymes, was co-ordinated by her and published by Kid's Own Publishing Partnership in 2001.

CONTENTS

Quintet:	Dead Men	11
	Firing Squad	12
	The Angelus	13
	Lir's Children	14
	Patriot Duties	15
Bás in Éirinn		16
The Resurrection		19
Scavenger		20
Song of the Settler's Wife		21
The Road to San Ysidro		22
Rescue		23
Four Letter Word		24
Love in the Rainy Season		25
Frost on the Roof		26
Yearning		27
Arabian Nights		28
Compromise		29
Lissadell		30
Song of Columba		32
A Foot on the Tide		34
Early Watch		35

Roscommon   36

Aluminium Shell   37

Over the Hudson River   38

Tá coiscéim coiligh ar an lá   39

Dry Days   40

Winter Solstice   41

Trainscape   42

Nesting   43

Maggie and the Crane-fly   44

Prodigal Daughters   46

Accommodation Policy   47

Mail-order Bride   48

The Poet of Silence   50

Nasturtiums 2001   51

Burning the Goalposts   52

Last Orders   53

Threshold   54

Holloway Boys   55

Keeping Jesus on the Cross   61

Rocky Point, North Carolina   63

Father Turning the Tables   64

Quintet

i
Dead Men

I played on Yeats' grave,
hunkered from my father's view,
a clutch of pebbles in my fist
to fire at the tombstone one by one
in a kind of prayer.

The wooden doors of Drumcliffe Church
are cast in shadow, cowled like a monk
they groan open wide enough
for the devil's arm to reel me in.

A new headstone marks my granda's grave.
It has no clever epitaph, just the number
nineteen thirty-five
and a dense silence.

Though all they had in common
was a graveside acquaintance
I linked the dead men in a tarnished chain
of local ore and stone I couldn't reconcile:

the vein of words that bled Ben Bulben
with insoluble barytes,
in each grain a scream, a tear,
a trickle of sweat in frenzied passion,

men and women loving, dying,
viscera compressed,
Diarmuid gored by the wild boar,
Patrick Branley grunting as he slants the spade.

ii
Firing Squad

Feverish you were and yearning,
filled with desire and a restless heart
– like mine, like mine –
that drove you from Glencar
into the struggle; from farming
to internment in a British camp,
prisoner of war. In between
you murdered one or two or even
ten soldiers of the Crown
before they broke your back
and let you go.

The ambulance stopped at Lugnagall
in nineteen thirty-five.
My father in his second week of school
was summoned to the gate where you
stood propped on sticks and leaning.
You had already said goodbye to wife
and newborn child, the toddler in the puddle
outside the house.
Now the other five stood facing you,
worse than any firing squad –
those trembling tears.

Your final words are framed
between the pillars of the gate:
Listen to your teachers.
Do what your mother says.

iii
The Angelus

Skipping in a circle holding hands,
The farmer wants a wife, we sang.
Red woollen stockings and brown laced shoes.
My mother was the teacher there. At noon
The angel of the Lord declared unto Mary
brown bottles of tea are warming by the stove.
The twisted paper stoppers are taken out
except for one my cousin has forgotten.
Behold the handmaid of the Lord
Be it done unto me according to
Like a bottle of champagne well shaken
the stopper pops and tea spews to the ceiling,
scalding legs, staining walls
and the Word was made Flesh.

iv

Lir's Children

Swans were her nearest neighbours.
They came pecking to her door
for the words she threw them,
butter on the crusts of bread.
Her children grown and scattered
sent her letters or came to see her,
their children by the hand in Sunday clothes.
Out and play and don't get dirty.

By the edge of Glencar lake
barytes sand would not retain
the shapes I moulded.
Castles fell in heaps.

v.

Patriot Duties

Kneeling for the rosary after lunch,
uniformed and surreptitious,
Teresa and I are reading Enid Blyton.
Sister Michael paces round the room,
preamble to the Rosary.

For the blind the sick the poor the lonely
get the British brutes out of the North.
A marvellous mix of politics and God.
She taught us 'Men behind the Wire'
and 'Come out ye Black and Tans'.

Sing that for your Granny, my father said
putting 10p for the missions
in my upturned palm.
She taught us Yeats' 'The Stolen Child'
and 'The Lake Isle of Innisfree',
coerced us into going to Feis Shiligh
as a patriotic duty.

They waxed the dampness in the cold Town Hall.
Hour after hour I gnawed on icepops,
rattled bags of crisps, booed the Donegal ones
whose mothers stood behind the judge
mouthing words and pulling strings of smiles.

I said 'The Stolen Child' in a small flat voice
tormented with a stutter.
I would have gone to live beneath the lake,
transformed into a staring otter.
I would have taken the cold forgetting comfort
they had to offer.

Bás in Éirinn

I see her by the range in the morning
rubbing long fingers stiffened overnight.
Her grey hair bun unfurled and plaited
reaches down her back.
She eats her breakfast from a cup
– a peeled and salted soft-boiled egg –
and drinks weak tea, lip
seeking out the rim to take a careful sip.
Her sorrowed face is waxen pale,
mouth laced tight in pain.
I tip-toe past her yet she hears
and reaches out to touch my head.

Good stock from Connemara –
farming people, stony faced.
Their hearts in every seed they planted,
a prayer in every bend to earth,
that crops might flourish
and the drudgery end.

The passage money came for her,
a woman of nineteen
unmonied and unmarried
she sailed from Cobh
to earn her dowry and return.

Seven years in Brooklyn,
seven years of toil,
the cooking and the cleaning,
shining silver for a millionaire.
Her mettle never wavered.
She scornfully refused
all New York could offer
for sweet yellow butter freshly churned,
the eye-stinging smoke of damp turf.

A match was made, a partnership
with a decent Mayo man.
Her dowry went to stock the byres,
a shire horse to pull the plough.
He built the house, grey stone on stone
as solid as himself.

Her kitchen flags were always swept,
above the fire the cáiscín baked
or a pot of washed potatoes boiled
for hungry men and pigs.
She spun the wool and knitted socks
for her husband and her sons,
sewed dresses for her daughters
in the yellow path of light
the oil-lamp gave.
The Rosary marked the end of day,
knees on the hard stone floor,
Sé do bheatha a Mhuire atá lán de grásta
elbows pressed on the wooden chairs,
Anois is ar uair ár mbáis Amen.

Her trunk in the attic
contained her treasure,
the store of seven years
preserved in camphor –
tablecloths, white sheets,
a little piece of silk, pink
and lovely to the touch,
a pair of boots high-heeled
and white, criss-cross laces
going in and out of twenty eyes.

I refused to witness death on her face
in the Galway morgue.
Candles burned by her coffin in the church,
a haze of incense to console,
heads bowed with black mantillas,
Granda sitting by the aisle,
his grief a damp and crumpled cloth,
a silent nod to *sorry for your trouble*
as the neighbours passed to shake his hand.

Her grave was lined with hailstones,
pearls in the dirt to welcome her
to eternal rest. Above the keeners' note
the priest intoned, *Go ndéana Dia trócaire uirthi.*
The Lord have mercy on her soul.

The Resurrection

for Loretta

Peeling potatoes
over Caheny's pub

listening to the radio
as the countdown began

I had lost you
in the wind chill
of absence

just as if
I was ringing
from some rural exchange

I heard you gasp
in Minnesota
as the Challenger exploded

over Cape Canaveral
a new grief stirred

as you stepped
from the tomb
my Lazarus

Scavenger

It's death's smell, he told me,
the furniture man,
Didn't you ever smell it before?
To me it was living like moon blood,
intimate and warm.

Generations of mice abide here,
evidence in every drawer,
dignity riddled with mouse shit.
Was it long before they
found you here?

Tincture of myrrh
in a brown glass bottle,
iodine and camphor ice,
sweet spirit of nitre couldn't save you
when the time came.

Two feet of the Virgin Mary in blue
in the corner of your room,
insurance for the afterlife.
Did you collect?
You gave no birth to a child of god

to vouchsafe your ascension.
Your polyester clothes are greasy
in my hands, plastic ivy unflappable
against your awful floral walls.
I'm searching for something of value

to steal, but you won't tell me
where the money is hidden.
I spit out your possessions in garbage bags:
public confession. Your sins are forgiven
by the waste disposal. Mine remain.

Song of the Settler's Wife

A patch of ground: a fork, a rake,
the instruments of cultivation.
We tore the earth from tap roots
tightly clinging to the soil
like a stone in a baby's fist,
until we shook it loose,
cast the remains on a compost heap
in double victory.
When the land was cleared
and raked to docile evenness
we planted twelve tomato plants
and marigolds to stand on guard.
Having satisfied our need to tinker
we shuffled home.

The Road to San Ysidro

In the dull oasis on the milpa
between San Ysidro and Alista
scrawny burros protest under wooden saddles,
bones protrude through grey backs.

Time dished out
in distant church-bell clangs.
La Gente live in one room shacks,
shuck corn in the open air.

Small dark children stare,
reach out their sticky hands
to finger gringas,
red mud on their bare feet.

They watch the snow-capped
mountain peaks smoke heavenward.
The volcanoes rest.
But for how long?

Rescue

My otter child with brown eyes
ragged on the water
and out of reach
never blinks.

Some awful wisdom rests
in her deadpan stare,
hints of wreckage
with buried gold
speckled in her eyes.

Four Letter Word

The clues laid across and down
remain roguishly unsolved.
Anagrams dangling, hints flung out
will not yield the right word,
ambiguous to the bitter end.
(White squares haunt me
with their cornered emptiness –
hospital beds in a darkened ward.)
If I had the answer
I could come unstuck.
Instead I hang from a four letter word
in painful uncertainty.

Love in the Rainy Season

These hard uneven walls
contain us in their blueness.
Tiny ants flit across the film of our frustration.
Jesus' feet have loosened from the cross,
meander to the side, even
He can't bear another aching sigh.

The rustle of your sleeping bag,
the spat of rain,
smells of burnt tortillas mingle
with the sweet waft of clothes
left soaking for too long like
love in the rainy season.

Across mud-spattered tiles
a radio plays to mock us.
The final blare of mariachi trumpets
is absurd.
My poor heart
Mi pobre corazon

Frost on the Roof

Leather-tongued with drink
the morning after
it's all right in talking but
you wouldn't want to be saying much
about yourself.

Frost on the roofs
in the afternoon
will not melt now.

Yearning

I need the sound
of the uilleann pipes –
raw escape of pain along the veins,
squeezing of air at the elbow,
the difficulty breathing.

Arabian Nights

Turbulence woke me.
The stallion pacing the paddock fence,
silver mane down his muscled neck,
pawing and snorting at the gate,
his cock as long as a baseball bat.

My sleeping dogs insisted
there were no intruders,
no Klu Klux Klan
burning crosses on the lawn,
unless they knew of them by day
and passed no judgement.

At the morning feed
we found Dolly on the loose,
prancing the grassy verge that led to the big house.
She came like a frightened child
for a bucket of oats.

Compromise

Sitting on plastic beach chairs
after midnight
watching over the garden wall
the gradual
eclipsing of the moon

our matching jackets buttoned
to the chin protect us

Lissadell

The barnacle geese in season
from October on
leave Greenland on a southern curve.
They navigate the skies and stay
all winter at Lissadell
in sanctuary. They used to say
the geese began as fish
birthed by the barnacle,
then turned fowl.

I have no season here,
no privileged duality.
I lack a myth that might protect me,
hunkered down in the smell of sea at low tide,
slipping fingers under moist and matted wrack,
picking mussels off a soft-furred rock.
Their lips are sealed.

Constance raced her chestnut mare
across the strand.
Eva picked mussels here with Esther.
Hand in salty hand we watch the sunset coaxing
light into another time.

The house is falling slowly down.
The name will die.
Perhaps some shrewd immigrant
with dollars from New York
will snap it up and start a health spa.
The local maids will trudge along the corridors
glad of the work. Saved from the ship.

It's summer now and the geese have gone.

Song of Columba

I am Columba, Prince of guilt,
surveying the death of Finian's troops
in the lengthening shadow of Ben Gulban.
Bodies strewn like the sheaves of a dismembered book
litter this field.
My victory is not sweet.

I will go to Inishmurray
where Molaise will hear my tale,
forgive my sins. I will take power from the cursing stones
to smite my foes.
Generations will pronounce my name
Saint Columba, man of letters, man of God.

I walked the waves from Streedagh
to the blessed rock glistening on the horizon –
a huge sea beetle foaming at the mouth.
Cormerants announced my feat, crying their sorrow
in an angry sky. Eider ducks dipped out of sight
into the belly of a rolling wave.

A council of shags stood on the rocks
whispering *Prince of guilt*.
The monks were at their evening prayer
singing *Glory*.

Once ashore I slept and dreamed
a voyage on a bitter sea,
north to the cold chastising wind,
a barren place and there to stay.

I am Columba, Prince of guilt,
walking the edge of cold Iona,
ancient with the weight of memory
turning with the days, grey.

A Foot on the Tide

My foot is on the Tide!
An unfrequented road –
Yet have all roads
A clearing at the end –

Emily Dickinson

After the sun set at Ballyconnell
we faltered over tilted ridges
like shipwrecked sailors dizzy at the knee.

I carried driftwood antlers
swept ashore,
ready for the next battle.

Scales whittled off made way for digit stumps.
White beached kelp fossils rising from grey stone,
the text of our first bruised landing.

Early Watch

Before the cloud of preoccupation descends
the fan heater is my radio.

My dog patters across the floor in the next room,
slumps down for the first nap.

My cat keeps the early watch
as I sip the first tea, extinguish the first fag.

The morning is as grey as the galvanised outhouse roof,
bleak as the crow's caw.

Roscommon

Crossing Tulsk you enter
big sky country
like Siberia on the radio
with far-flung peasants.

A woman carries a white plastic bucket,
her other hand in her apron pocket –
fetching water?
feeding hens?

A Morris Minor pulls
out of an invisible road.
We slow from 45 to 30,
processing for miles behind it.

Huge hands grip the steering.
A grey face under a peaked cap.
I notice as I pass
the sky still floating over golden sedge.

Aluminium Shell

The caravan door ajar,
a piece of elastic looped
through the hole
where the lock should have been.
No one there except a black dog
guarding broken toys and a plastic bottle.

When I found them in,
crammed in the back were faces
indistinguishable in the evening light,
hands round mugs of tea,
the only heat from four gas rings
circulated by the draft from the missing lock.

I imagine them at night
sleeping in their tumbled beds,
the elastic wound round the long nail,
the door closed tight,
keeping in their world.

Over the Hudson River
for Maeve O'Beirne

When they saw
skyscrapers in Manhattan,
towers of glinting glass,
did they remember the reflection
of the sun on the mercury-flooded fields
in Gurteen and Kilavill?
The paddy fields of Coleman Country
spawned reels, not rice.

Over the Hudson River
staring down the bridge
along taut metal strings
did they hear the snipe?

Tá coiscéim coiligh ar an lá

The cock's a mathematician,
self-appointed master
whose final two-inch step elongates
the evening light
tá coiscéim coiligh ar an lá

cock of the walk
he struts and circling quivers,
slows the setting sun
for the rallentando, one step dance
tá coiscéim coiligh ar an lá

Dry Days

We leave our coats on
like him and settle
into upright wooden chairs.

He shuffles round
to change the plug
from telly to the heater,

plonks wine
on the red formica table,
fetches three wine glasses

misted with the greasy prints
of our last visit,
cobwebbed if it's been a month.

The range is cold forever
and he no longer sees
the lino's bitten back.

Our talk comes out in clouds
of weather, a steady drip
from the leaking roof
that can't be fixed 'til the dry days come.

Winter Solstice
from a painting by Bruegel

Sockless, the elders sit,
backs to the sea, in the quiet
company of dogs.
Viva la virgen del buen viaje!
White graffiti on the harbour cliffs.

High up, we tourists
on the windy terrazzo
of the Vaca Azul
watch the sun go down
in the African sea.

As the next shift of elders
arrives – the three wise men –
we order beer and speculate,
while Mary slips
into Bethlehem, unnoticed.

Trainscape

soft bog cotton blunts
the rushy field

a solitary tree leans
to the ground

in a way
I can almost forgive

the colour is washed
from an empty sky

knuckles press
against raw skin

the fuchsia bleeds
down a whitewashed wall

and I can almost forgive
the unfathomable sameness

the ignorant stump
of a stone wall

Nesting

We bought the painting on the never-never,
trusting we would get the house
of solid blue limestone,
walls a foot thick,
impossible to drill.

The red deal floor was laid
the year that I was born
by a man who fought with Con in Stephen's Green.
Savouring the fire we sit on the leaking chairs
my father stole for us.

Our lease from the Gore-Booths
for nine hundred years
is the perfect answer for the children of Lir.
We have been in exile.
Now we're home.

Maggie and the Crane-fly

from your fractured web
you gave me a gift –
a small gossamer-ringed hole
of memory

A shrewd million legs
upon the window
enlaced in a map
of seasonal slaughter.

You remembered
the crane-fly found
on the sodden tea bag,
wings glued,

clapped together like oars
on reaching the shore.
You placed it on the sill,
hoping for a miracle,

feeling the burden
of decision
pull you towards assistance,
the hoover in your hand.

The crane-fly sat astride
the narrow nozzle,
refusing the seduction
of drowning in dust,

chose instead to tumble
in cold dishwater.

You felt the death for hours
that wingless, useless,
chastened day.

Prodigal Daughters

Giddy with the hopes
of making honey,
we pledged ourselves
to hopeless causes.

Like bees, we swarmed home,
slipping in back doors quietly,
saying nothing of where we'd been.

We were greeted cautiously.
Fears stirred we might reveal
why we had left.

We stayed,
having learnt new dances,
donning the shackles
like bracelets,

drinking our own wine,
not expecting fatted calves –
mistresses of biding time.

Accommodation Policy

They used to say
there were more Wards
on Connaughton Road
than in the hospital.

Now there are seventy-four boulders
to keep them out

and space enough
for the city fathers
to crawl under.

Mail-order Bride

JFK to Heathrow,
new life on the Virgin Express,

a bag of clothes, the guitar and $40
when the dollar was weak.

You left blue money
in the top pine drawer,

the clippings of tin
from your still life.

Strike a pose and
freeze for hours.

My job to warm you
when you came home.

Fitou and casseroles
every night and the moon

there when you opened the window.
Sirens and trains, the heavy metal

hum in all our phone calls
that long September.

I shouldn't have mentioned
the hurricane.

You joked about the flat
being small;

you could lie
    with your head in the kitchen
        legs in the sitting room
            hands in the hall.

The Poet of Silence

His dream was to play the violin.
At seventeen he stopped.

I had no instrument
He gave as explanation

Adding
     in Russia
There is no lost and found.

Nasturtiums 2001
for Basho

They didn't grow 'til August
when the second clutch
of swallow eggs

had hatched
and new leaf buds
appeared on the cherry tree.

By the equinox
the world had changed

but they stayed under
the rose hips

far across enemy lines.

Burning the Goalposts

for Helen Byrne

We were goalies that day
in a game gone mad

with both sides united
against us

let them score
their own goals

as we walked
off the pitch together

through the turnstiles
in search of a new game

with no rules nor referee
no penalties nor points

let's burn the goalposts slowly
and warm our aching hands

refund the blind spectators
turn the pitches into parks

Last Orders

for Leland Bardwell

tobacco-coloured ferns dip
into the November fog
of my full headlights

delighted
your square fingers close
round vodka and coke

like that poker glee
of scooping
the final pot

in the sky
the planet
that will take you home

Threshold

As well as the house being damp
the coat had a dual role.

The unwelcome caller met
on the threshold was told
she was on her way out,

the wanted guest that
she had just come in.

What intrigues me is who
was on which list –

farmers with their mute attentions
for a handsome widow,

headscarved women prying
for flakes of gossip in the fire?

And when she was just going out
where did she go?

I see her striding to the north
with the lake on her right,

heading for the Leitrim border,
her coat pulled tight.

Holloway Boys
for R. Pearce

1.
He came all hours
when it wasn't his time

and when it was, I followed him
along dark corridors

pleading, *Put your cigarettes away
come back.*

2.
He scared me early on
with his piercing love,

made me feel as useless
as he was lost.

Astride the small partition,
screaming *Oh me bollocks.*

3.
Boys congregated
on the back stairs

for lessons in humiliation,
piss and spit and dope.

Someone flicked a lighter
outside my room.

A Philip Larkin look-a-like
lost control again

in the class next door –
the boys were baiting.

4.
Sometimes he sucked his thumb,
talked of down the flats,

self-defence and GBH,
spray-paint and nicking cars.

He knew every nuance of rejection.

5.
He came to the staff room door
and threatened to have me fired

for not catching him out on bunking off,
said he'd left me messages.

I fed his rage with cakes and tea,
apologised, gave him my number.

6.
I had left London by the time he phoned
Hello Richard this is miss.

There's always one who breaks your heart
and clouds of gulls swoop down

on the playground after lunch.

Keeping Jesus on the Cross

1.
We were asked to Gillen's Station
by the handsome son, the ring
in his eyebrow seemed tender.

We sat with the neighbours
we had never met, on the Friday
after Easter,

belted out the prayers we knew,
nodded at the gospel, felt safe
with the good Samaritan tone

until the Post Communion prayers
Wash me water
Streaming from his side.

The priest's favourite –
Jesus hanging from the cross,
as if the story never ended.

2.
Oh Jesus dear Jesus
is it really very bad?

You brought it on yourself
with the company you kept.

People talked about the hippies
and the trollop

and your poor mother –
what you put her through.

This is our addiction
to exquisite pain.

Don't get off the cross just yet.
We really need your dying.

Rocky Point, North Carolina

Are the tree frogs sawing
through the turgid nights?

Is the water snake still hiding
under the trellised steps?

Do the dogwoods sing
in the hurricane winds?

Do the buzzards
keep their distance?

Does the wolf spider lurk
in the dark pump house?

Is the grey marle track
still leaden underfoot

as it leads to the hickory grove
and the swamp of spiny ferns

jungled over, bushwhacked
and abandoned?

Father Turning the Tables

He taught me how to learn
my Irish spellings
rapping out a rhythm
on the kitchen table
no-fada-im-e-fada-ad

He asked me to teach him
long division and I did
explaining about tables turning
and how sometimes
things don't work out evenly

he knew about that